A Guide to the Gracious Old Homes, Churches and C
of Beaufort, South Carolina

HISTORIC BEAUFORT

PUBLISHED BY HISTORIC BEAUFORT FOUNDATION, INC.

HISTORIC BEAUFORT FOUNDATION

Inspired by his participation in Beaufort's first preservation effort on "The Committee for the Preservation of the Lafayette Building," Howard E. Danner, in 1967, directed the organizing of this foundation, which is a monument to his unflagging interest and energy.

Under the direction of Dr. Carl Feiss, architect and former director of the National Trust for Historic Preservation, and his associate Russell Wright of Washington, D.C., the Foundation made a complete inventory and study of historic and architecturally important buildings in that part of Beaufort which is now listed on the National Register of Historic Places as a National Landmark. Subsequently, it has published its fourth edition of its guidebook, has taken an active part in the preservation of eight important houses that were in danger of demolition, and has restored and partly furnished its John Mark Verdier House as a house museum.

The Foundation has capital assets in the form of a revolving fund and it owns and operates the John Mark Verdier House, in which its headquarters are housed.

Membership in Historic Beaufort Foundation is open to all who are in sympathy with its purpose.

To the visitors to Beaufort: we hope that this book will make it easy for you to find the many attractions our community offers. To the Beaufort residents: we urge you to treat yourselves as visitors and to use this book to rediscover your own city. We promise that you will be more proud of it than ever.

The Trustees of
Historic Beaufort Foundation, Inc.
801 Bay Street, Beaufort, South Carolina

Table of Contents

Fifth Edition 1985

Printed by Kennickell Printing Co, Savannah, Ga.

A Brief History of Beaufort

When Port Royal Sound was named, William Shakespeare had not been born; the Spanish Armada had not sailed against England; and "Santa Elena" had not yet become "St. Helena."

The following "history" will give the visitor a backward glance of Old World contact and New World conflict out of which has come this sun-drenched, pleasant place.

The Spaniards

In 1520, less than thirty years after Columbus discovered America, Captain Francisco Gordillo, exploring from Hispaniola, stopped near Port Royal Sound long enough to name the region Santa Elena, one of the oldest European place names in America.

In 1559, to prevent the intrusion of the French, and to protect the galleon route from Havana to Cadiz, Philip II of Spain ordered a colony planted at Santa Elena. Angel Villafane explored the Sea Islands but failed to establish a permanent colony.

The French

In 1562 Admiral Coligny of France sent Captain Jean Ribaut to found a colony of French Protestants in the New World. Ribaut explored the coast from Florida to South Carolina and decided upon the sea islands of Santa Elena. He described the areas as a place teeming with edible wild life and with a harbor where "all the shippes of the world" could anchor in comfort. He named the harbor Port Royal, a name which has been in continuous use for over four hundred years.

Ribaut left thirty Protestants on modern Parris Island at his settlement of Charlesfort (named for the infant king of France) and returned to France for supplies. Religious wars detained him, and his thirty colonists, plagued by troubles with the Indians and among themselves, abandoned Charlesfort, built a boat on Parris Island, and sailed for France. After hunger and thirst had reduced them to cannibalism the survivors were rescued and returned to France.

In 1564, Ribaut, undeterred, returned to the southern coasts, this time to the St. Johns River in Florida, where he established Fort Caroline.

The Spaniards Again

The alarmed Spaniards quickly sent Pedro Menendez de Aviles to counter the French. Menendez founded St. Augustine and from this base ruthlessly eliminated the French colony, killing Ribaut and the entire garrison. Menendez then established a string of posts along the coasts of Florida, Georgia and South Carolina. The northernmost of these was placed on the site of Ribaut's Charlesfort on Parris Island.

In 1566 the Spaniards built the fort, San Phillipe and the Mission of Santa Elena at Port Royal. In 1577 a larger fort, San Marcos, replaced San Phillipe, destroyed following an Indian massacre. For twenty years, until 1586, the Spaniards fought off Indian uprisings and French buccaneers, and continued their explorations and missionary works, reaching inland as far as Tennessee. By 1580 the settlement was one of the largest Spanish towns north of Mexico. But more troubles lay ahead.

In 1586 the English privateer, Sir Francis Drake, attacked and burned St. Augustine, forcing withdrawal of outlying Spanish forces and the final abandonment of the settlement at Port Royal. But for another hundred years Port Royal was Spanish lands and waters, and intruders ventured in at their peril.

The English

In the 1600's the English began to appear among the Sea Islands, looking for a site for a colony. William Hilton came in 1663, followed by Robert Sandford in 1666. Sandford left behind South Carolina's first settler, Dr. Henry Woodward, to minister to the Indians. Woodward was captured by the Spaniards but escaped and returned with the original colonists in 1670. When ships carrying the first settlers for South Carolina arrived at Port Royal, Woodward and the Indians warned the immigrants that the Spanish claim and threat were too strong for contest. The settlers moved north and settled the banks of the Ashley River in 1670.

By the 1700's English planters and traders had established a foothold at Port Royal. The two most prominent men were Thomas Nairn on St. Helena Island and John Barnwell on Port Royal Island. These men were mainly responsible for founding the town of Beaufort in 1711.

The Scots

In 1685 Henry Erskine, Lord Cardross, settled a small band of Scots Covenanters on Spanish Point. They called their settlement Stuart Town. They made the mistake of encouraging the Yemassee Indians to raid and plunder the Spanish villages in Florida. In retailiation the Spaniards, in 1686, scattered the settlement and burned Stuart Town.

The Yemassee

On Easter Sunday, 1715, the fierce Yemassee tribe, aided by the Creeks from Georgia and Alabama, attacked and burned the young town of Beaufort, torturing and killing many settlers. Others escaped to a ship anchored in the bay. John Barnwell rallied the Port Royal Militia and helped Governor Craven drive the Yemassee into Florida from where they continued to raid the Sea Islands until 1728.

The Swiss

In 1733 a group of Swiss immigrants, led by Jean Pierre Purry, settled the town of Purrysburg on the Savannah River. This settlement, along with the founding of Georgia, gave considerable security to the Beaufort area.

The Crops

The fresh water swamps of the mainland produced the most profitable South Carolina crop, rice. In the 1740's Eliza Lucas and Andre De Veaux developed the second most important export crop, indigo, from which blue dye was derived. Indigo was perfectly suited for the Sea Islands and was the primary cash crop in the two decades prior to the Revolution.

The Government

The Parish system was the political basis for colonial South Carolina. The Beaufort area had four parishes which sent representatives to the Commons House of Assembly: St. Helena, among the Sea Islands (1712); Prince William, on the mainland (1745); St. Peter, along the Savannah (1747); and St. Luke, south of the Broad River (1767). The Parish Vestry was the only effective body of local government.

Prosperity and Politics

The production and export of indigo and a large shipbuilding industry in the Sea Islands brought prosperity to Port Royal, and the occupation of St. Augustine by the British made the area more attractive to settlers. The population had increased to approximately 4,000 on the eve of the Revolution.

The four parishes of the area began to vie with the Charleston parishes for political influence. An attempt by the royal governor, Lord Charles Greville Montague, to move the capitol to Port Royal (the Beaufort Assembly of 1772) was listed by Thomas Jefferson as one of the grievances in the Declaration of Independence. Opinion in Beaufort was sharply divided over Revolution. Thomas Heyward, Jr. of St. Luke's Parish was the most prominent Patriot, while the powerful De Veaux family led the substantial Loyalist support for the king.

Revolution

Beaufort played no major role in the early years of the Revolution, but as British hopes for success faded in New York and Pennsylvania they looked southward, and in December, 1778, captured and occupied Savannah. Early in the New Year General Prevost sent H. M. S. Vigilant with two hundred and fifty troops aboard to capture Beaufort. They landed at Laurel Bay and marched toward Beaufort but were intercepted and repulsed near the present Marine Air Station by General William Moultrie with three hundred militia. The British returned to their ship but the Americans were forced to abandon the defense of Port Royal Island because the small garrison at Fort Lyttleton, guarding Beaufort, had spiked the guns and blown up the fort on the approach of the seventy-four gun ship-of-the-line, *Vigilant*.

The next month, Prevost attempted, with near success, to capture Charleston but was forced to retreat down the coast, finally occupying Beaufort in July, 1779. In October the siege of Savannah by American troops and the French West Indies fleet forced the British to evacuate Beaufort. Charleston fell to the British in 1780. During its occupation (1780-82) the King's Highway to Savannah was guarded by the British Fort Balfour at Coosawhatchie.

In the Beaufort area, bitter rivalries led to scattered fighting between Tories and Patriots. Colonel John Laurens, son of Henry Laurens and close friend of Alexander Hamilton, was killed near the Combahee River in one of the last skirmishes of the Revolutionary War.

Cotton

The Beaufort District was ruined by the war and recovery was slow. But in the early 1790's a new crop was introduced from the Bahamas, via Georgia, which was to form the basis of the greatest era of prosperity and influence in the town's long history. This was Sea Island Cotton, the finest and most expensive cotton grown in America. In the years between 1790 and 1860 cotton produced so many men of wealth and influence that one historian described Beaufort as the "wealthiest, most aristocratic and cultivated town of its size in America." Some of Beaufort's more prominent citizens in the antebellum era were Senator Robert W. Barnwell, Secretary of the Navy Paul Hamilton, Congressman and poet William J. Grayson, and Senator Robert Barnwell Rhett, the "father of Seccession."

This was the period when most of the fine homes which give distinction to Beaufort's National Historic District were built. During this period also, Beaufort gained the reputation for having some of the finest libraries and some of the best preparatory schools in the South. The most notable of these was the Beaufort College whose building, erected in 1852, now houses the branch campus of the University of South Carolina.

Civil War and the End to Opulence

With the opening of the Civil War the Sea Island cotton kingdom came to a swift and thunderous end. On November 7, 1861, Commodore Samuel DuPont led a flotilla of U. S. Navy warships into Port Royal Sound and quickly reduced the half finished Confederate forts, Walker and Beauregard, permanently securing the Sea Islands for the Union. The planters with their families fled inland, abandoning their homes, lands and slaves. Beaufort became the chief base of the South Atlantic blockading squadron and headquarters of the U. S. Army, Department of the South. The great houses served as hospitals, and as offices and quarters for the military and were thus saved for other generations. During the occupation by Union troops, Quaker missionaries founded the Penn School for black freedmen on St. Helena Island.

After the War — Forward

Returning whites found their property and lands virtually confiscated under the Direct Tax Laws. Few of them ever regained what had been lost. During the Occupation years, agriculture became almost non-existent and in 1865 one observer wrote that the Beaufort region, formerly one of the most highly cultivated portions of the globe, "was not raising enough food to last until spring." The more enterprising and tough-minded adapted quickly and began the long struggle back from crushing defeat and reprisal. Cotton production recovered but it never regained its supremacy, and with the coming of the boll weevil about 1919, the great long-fibered cotton disappeared forever from the Sea Islands.

In 1893 a giant storm came out of the Atlantic leaving destruction in its wake. The hurricane came ashore at the high tide, piling water on water until all of the islands were inundated and swept clean of existing agriculture and shipping. Many thousands were drowned and a phosphate mining operation was stopped permanently. Like war, it has remained a reference point in the region's history.

Where rice, indigo and cotton once flourished, feed crops, vegetables and soybeans, with attendant livestock production, supply the agricultural wealth. The shrimp fleet "drags" the sounds and coastal waters and a seafood industry thrives.

New, clean manufacturing and large military installations add greatly to the economy of the area.

A fast-growing tourist "industry" brings in new dollars, and retired people, drawn by the climate, the history and the, as yet, unspoiled beauty, are new settlers who add to the intellectual and cultural life in the Sea Islands.

Meanwhile an energetic and growing number of preservationists fight bravely, and often successfully, to keep the houses and scenes that make Beaufort an unusual, "different" place.

The Foundation is indebted to the University of South Carolina, Beaufort Branch and the Beaufort County Historical Society for providing the source from which most of this "history" was condensed.

Map Legend

1 — Sheldon Camp, 1776-1780
2 — Purrysburg American Militia Camp 1779
British Gen. Prevost Landed Apr. 29, 1779
3 — Battle — 1779 Fort Balfour 1780-1783
4 — American Lookout Post 1779-1780
5 — Port Royal Ferry Post 1779
6 — Battle of Port Royal Island Feb. 3, 1779
7 — Salt Creek Bridge Post 1779
8 — Fort Lyttleton
9 — Grave of Thomas Heyward

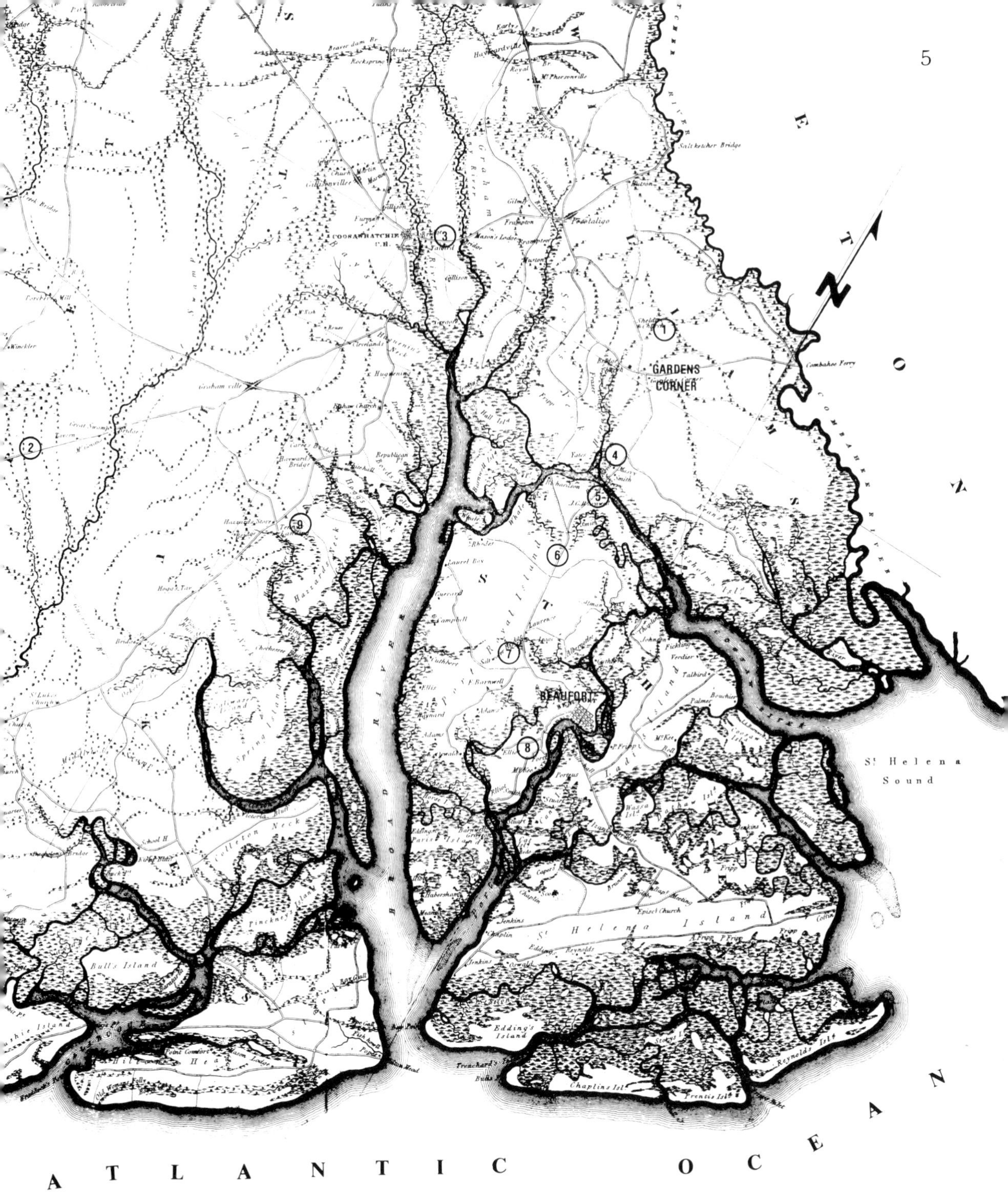
ATLANTIC OCEAN
St Helena Sound
BEAUFORT
GARDENS CORNER
COOSAWHATCHIE C.H.
Pocotaligo
Saltketcher Bridge
Combahee Ferry
Grahamville
Gillisonville
McPhersonville
Colleton Neck
Spring Island
Pinckney's Island
Bull's Island
Hilton Head
Point Comfort
St Helena Island
Edding's Island
Chaplins Isl
Reynolds Isld
Frentis Isl
Parris Island
Port Royal Island
Ladies Island
Hall Isld
1
2
3
4
5
6
7
8
9

Introduction to Beaufort Architecture

The community which is now Beaufort had its beginning in 1710, when Barbadian planters, English indenture servants, tradesmen, and religious dissenters came here to seek their fortunes. These early settlers built houses of clapboard and of tabby, a durable cement-like material composed of oyster shells, sand, and a lime obtained through the burning of oyster shells. As prosperity increased, the houses grew larger and more elaborate. Designed for airiness and coolness, the "Beaufort Style" incorporated elements of Georgian and Colonial architecture as well as those of Greek Revival and semi-tropical Spanish. House building in Beaufort reached its peak during the years 1820-1860. During and after the Civil War, the houses were sold at auction by the Federal Government. Only a very few of the original owners were able to reclaim their homes. Several were bought by former slaves, some by former Union soldiers, and several by Northerners who came to Beaufort as participants in the Reconstruction effort.

The "Beaufort Style" is a convenient but rather general classification as no one particular house incorporates all of its characteristics. It differs from the more urban designs of Charleston and Savannah in that the Beaufort house is free standing on a large lot, frequently a formal garden, and is oriented to take full advantage of the prevailing southwesterly breezes. It more nearly resembles the plantation house, brought to town, as some indeed were, and adapted to the summer heat and the dampness of the lowcountry.

Raised high on a sturdy foundation of stucco over brick or tabby, the Beaufort house is characterized by a two-story piazza, frequently extending partially around both sides of the house. There are notable exceptions to this as in the case of Marshlands, where the piazza is only one story, or where the piazza is limited to a two story portico over the front entrance and a balcony immediately above, as in the case of the John Mark Verdier House, Tabby Manse and Tidewater. The classic orders or variations thereof are frequently used for the columns, an excellent example being the Milton Maxcy or Secession House where Ionic capitals are used on the first level of columns, and Corinthian capitals are found on the second story. The piazzas are supported by stuccoed piers or arches, usually left open for ventilation. Exterior stairways are most frequently centered, but may be just as effectively located to one side as in the John Joyner Smith house and, again, in the Milton Maxcy house.

The main core of the house is usually T-shaped with chimneys inset or on the exterior side walls. The roof is low-pitched and inconspicuous. The typical floor plan provides central hallways on both the main and upper floors with an impressive stairway to the rear. Frequently there is a handsome Palladian window at the landing. There may be a garden entrance directly opposite the main entrance.

Ceiling heights, which range from fourteen to eighteen feet on the main floor, ornamental woodwork such as paneling, wainscoting, mantels and cornices, all combine to create an effect of elegance, airiness, and light. In the later homes, cornices and ceiling medallions are of elaborately molded plaster from which chandeliers of exceptional quality may be suspended.

Fireplaces and mantels have been given varied treatment. Several are noted for Adam-style decoration. In some of the later houses there was a vogue for mantels of imported Italian marble, and in the Joseph Johnson house and in Marshlands one finds an attractive use of 17th century Delft Tiles.

The total impression gained is that of a community of affluence, taste and cultivation but with a measure of restraint. A Northern visitor of around 1850 described Beaufort society as follows.

> *"Nothing in our largest cities can equal the display of carriages and equipages which, with the servants in livery, may be seen on a pleasant afternoon, when the mothers and daughters of these cotton lords take their accustomed airing."*

Although, as you walk through the National Historic Landmark District, you will be more apt to encounter a Ford or Volkswagen than a Surrey or Brougham, you can readily imagine how these homes appeared more than a century ago. We can be grateful that they have escaped "progress' and are still with us as continuing symbols of a gracious society.

The Tours

The best way to see and enjoy the lovely old homes and churches of Beaufort is on foot, which would allow you to stop and chat with those residents you might chance to see in the yards. However, we have prepared for you two driving tours to prevent your missing any part through the press of time.

Whether you begin "up town" with house No. 1 or at the bridge with house No. 32, you can drive over the historic district in a matter of minutes. We urge you to do it all; then come back and walk it at your leisure.

Begin the Town Tour at the Chamber of Commerce at Charles and Bay Streets.

TOWN TOUR

1. 1001 Bay Street

The George Elliott House
circa 1840

When George Elliott built this house about 1840, it had no upper verandah; so the four massive pillars rose to the roof unimpeded. The second story verandah was added in the late nineteenth century. Among the many excellent features of the house are a fine fanlit doorway, attractive iron railings, and good interior details including marble mantels, gilded cornices and moldings.

Dr. W. A. Jenkins, who owned over 1500 slaves and was one of the richest men in Beaufort, bought the house before the Civil War. He fled at the outbreak of the war, leaving behind him a valuable collection of books and furniture. When he returned in 1865, Dr. Jenkins found his belongings had been moved to Hilton Head Island. Jenkins went to Hilton Head, identified and reclaimed his valuables, and brought them back to Beaufort on a barge. His house was sold in 1866 by the Federal Government for taxes and was bought by George Holmes.

The above house has been beautifully restored as a house museum and is well worth seeing.

2. 807-813 Bay Street

The John Cross Tavern Site

John Cross, who is mentioned in St. Helena's vestry book in 1802, had his Tavern on this site in the 1700's. The Tavern occupied two buildings separated by a driveway leading to the John Cross dock. The Township Council, in the late 1700's, made the driveway permanent.

The Taproom and kitchen occupied one side of the divided structure, with the owner's living quarters above. The other side contained sleeping quarters with a ladies' retiring room on the second floor. The two buildings were connected by an overhead walkway across the drive.

The John Cross Tavern, being the only one in the Township, entertained many famous guests, among them John Wesley, the English founder of Methodism, in 1735. Parson Weems, originator of the Washington "Cherry Tree" story, died here later in the century. Pirates also paid the tavern an occasional visit from their rendezvous on Fripp Island.

Today a tavern under the original name occupies the upper floor of one side (above another restaurant), while an attractive book shop occupies the other side.

3. 802-806 Bay Street

The Habersham House

circa 1800

Built by a Mr. Rhodes in the late eighteenth or early nineteenth century and sold to John Habersham, this fine stucco building of excellent proportions is thought to have been at different times a custom house, a hotel, and a commissary store during the Civil War. On the upper floors it has the remains of a beautiful circular staircase, wide floor boards, and fine woodwork.

In the old days, the front yard, down to the water, was a beautiful garden. Near it was the shipyard of Rhodes and Talbird, where ships were built for the War of 1812.

5. 713 Craven Street

The Arsenal

1795-1852

Built in 1795 on the site of Beaufort's first courthouse and rebuilt in 1852, this castellated, Gothic, pseudo-military style structure has pointed Gothic windows, heavy fortress-like walls, and a massive pointed arch gateway.

The Beaufort Volunteer Artillery (now Det 1, Troop B, 713th Armd Cavalry Regiment) was organized in April, 1775 and is the fifth oldest military unit in the United States. It has taken part in every war fought by this nation, including the Revolutionary War. For years it was housed in or connected with the Beaufort Arsenal.

The two brass trophy guns captured from the British in 1779 were seized by Union soldiers at the fall of Fort Walker in 1861 and returned to Beaufort after 1880.

The Arsenal now houses a small but interesting museum of local memorabilia.

6. 901 Craven Street

The W. J. Jenkins House

circa 1850

Although the present two-story portico is thought to have replaced an earlier verandah, this house is still a good example of the well-designed, finely proportioned Beaufort-style house. Amazingly, four of the five fan lights are the originals, delicately cut glass in a Venetian pattern.

During the Civil War the house was occupied by Union troops, and afterward it became a boarding house. Today it is privately owned.

7. 907 Craven Street

The Tabernacle Baptist Church

1800's

This picturesque white clapboard church with its tall belltower and red-roofed steeple was built in the 1800's by the Beaufort Baptist Church. "The Tabernacle" was used as a meeting house and lecture room. At the close of the War Between the States about 500 black members withdrew from the Baptist Church and bought the Tabernacle.

The present church was organized in 1863 by the Reverend Solomon Peck of Boston.

Greatly damaged by the storm of 1893, a great part of the church was rebuilt following the original style.

The grave and a bust of Robert Smalls (1839-1915), first a slave, then Captain of the "Planter," and later U.S. Congressman, are in the churchyard.

8. 1009 Craven Street

The Thomas Rhett House

circa 1820

Similar to the "Secession House," this is an excellently proportioned house with two-story wraparound piazzas and transom-lighted doorways. The fine interior is accented by an arch of carved palmetto fans over the central hall. Recent renovations revealed beautiful original mantels in the two principal front rooms.

The builder of the house is unknown; however, Thomas Rhett, with his wife Caroline Barnwell, daughter of Edward Barnwell, lived here prior to the Civil War. He was the oldest of seventeen Smith children who changed their name to Rhett in honor of their great-great grandfather, William Rhett, whose family name had died out.

This house which for a number of years was an inn recently has been beautifully restored as a private home.

9. 1109 Craven Street

William Fickling House. "The Rectory"
Early 1800's

Built by William Fickling, this two-story clapboard house with Adam-style interior is now the Rectory of St. Helena's Episcopal Church. The grounds extend through to North Street and give a view across the lawn of the beautiful south gate of the church.

William Fickling, who taught in a boys' school, lived here with his wife, Sarah Johnson, and the earliest known record of the house is 1807, when Mrs. Fickling, after her husband's death, sold the property.

Just prior to the Civil War, the house was owned by a Rhett whose brothers owned the Thomas Rhett House and Secession House on the same street.

The original house was only one room deep. The rear portion, including a bay window on the east, was added after the Civil War. Photographs made by the Federal Government show an ell, with chimneys at the rear. Both front rooms on the first level are paneled up to the window sills with two-foot wide boards. The interior also features black marble mantels and wide heart-pine boards on the floor.

10. 1113 Craven Street

The Milton Maxcy House. "Secession House." circa 1813

This fine example of the "Beaufort Style" has excellent proportions.

The lot on which the Secession House stands was granted to Robert Williams around 1743. It is said that a tabby house stood there before the Revolution.

Around 1800 Milton Maxcy came to Beaufort from Massachusetts to open a school for boys and acquired the property. He removed the tabby second floor, and added two stories of wood siding.

The next owner, Edmund Rhett, rebuilt the two upper floors completely, circa 1861, using modified Greek Revival architecture.

An inscription on the basement wall reads: "In this house the first meeting of Secession was held in South Carolina." The Beaufort County Delegation met in the east room to support South Carolina's secession. The delegates went directly to the boat landing and set off for Charleston to cast their ballots for secession.

This dwelling was used by the Union Army for headquarters of General Rufus Saxton, billeting of officers, a hospital, and for the office of Paymaster.

Turn right on Church St.

11. 501 Church Street

St. Helena's Episcopal Church
1724

The church was built in 1724, for a parish organized in 1712; the building has been enlarged twice. Its tottering steeple, which is said to have been 118 feet high, was removed in 1866. The present steeple was erected in 1942. Constructed of brick, much of which came from England as ships' ballast, and finished in smooth cement stucco, the church has excellent exterior proportions. The interior contains some fine colonial detail, as evidenced in the simple columns, the elaborate cornices, and the delicate balustrade of the slave gallery.

In 1734 Captain John Bull, whose wife was massacred by the Yemassee Indians, gave silver to the church in her memory. The Bull chalice, paten and alms basin are still used by St. Helena's on special occasions.

During the Civil War, Federal troops dismantled the church and used it as a hospital, uprooting slabs from the graveyard for operating tables. The present altar was donated by the sailors of the *U.S.S. New Hampshire*, which was stationed here after the Civil War.

One of the first persons to be buried in the churchyard was Colonel John Barnwell, better known as "Tuscarora Jack." After leading successful raids against the troublesome Tuscarora Indians, Barnwell died in 1724. His grave, along with others, lies beneath the twice-enlarged church.

Buried here are two Confederate Generals. Lt. General Richard H. Anderson, a West Pointer who resigned to serve the Confederacy was with the South Carolina Brigade and fought at Williamsburg, Virginia. Brigadier General Stephen Elliott was Captain of the Beaufort Volunteer Artillery and the Charleston Battalion. He was sent to Virginia, made a Brigadier General and was wounded while defending Petersburg.

Two British officers, killed in a skirmish near Port Royal during the Revolution, were buried by Captain John Barnwell on the right side of the brick walk on the west side. Barnwell sent his sergeant into the church for a prayer book, read the burial service, and then said, "We have shown the British we not only can best them in battle, but that we can also give them a Christian burial."

Dr. Perry feared being buried alive. He had his slaves build his tomb and made his friends promise to provision it with a loaf of bread, a jug of water, and an axe so that in case he awakened after burial, he could refresh himself while hacking his way out.

In the parish house grounds, north side, are the graves of persons who, because of death from dueling or suicide, were not allowed burial in hallowed ground. While excavation for a heating system for the parish house was in progress, a common grave containing twenty-five skeletons was found, but no records.

St. Helena's parish has been in continuous religious activity since 1712 and is one of the oldest living churches in the United States.

Turn right on Prince

12. 600 Charles Street

Baptist Church of Beaufort

1844

The Baptist Church is an excellent example of the Greek Revival period, and is said by several outstanding authorities to be one of the finest in America. The exterior walls are finished in white stucco with high, many-paned windows. On the east front is a recessed portico with two plain Doric columns resting on sandstone blocks set in the flagstone floor. Over the porch is a simple pediment extending the width of the building. From the roof rises the square tower surmounted by an octagonal spire, which was added in the mid-twentieth century.

The beautifully proportioned interior has a gallery on three sides, supported by fluted Doric columns. The cove ceiling has unusually fine plaster ornamentation which was made by some of the highly skilled slave artisans of the era. The band of leaves which surrounds the whole ceiling, the rosettes and paterae which make up most of the decorations are probably the finest plaster work in Beaufort. The whole interior has a simplicity and dignity that are restful as well as beautiful.

In 1795 Henry Holcombe of the Euhaw Church moved to Beaufort where a small building was built for the branch of Euhaw here. Probably this building was on the present site of the Baptist Church. The church grew and in 1804 the Baptist Church of Beaufort was constituted.

A great revival began in October 1831 with the coming of Reverend Daniel Baker, a Presbyterian evangelist. Hundreds professed conversion. The revival gave four ministers to the Episcopal Church and Richard Fuller to the Baptist Church. During the pastorate of Richard Fuller the present building was erected. The Tabernacle Church on Craven Street was used as a lecture room and for evening worship. In 1857 the slave membership was 3317 while the white members numbered 182. During the Civil War, the church (like so many other buildings in Beaufort) was used as a hospital.

Continue on Prince

13. 901 Prince Street

The Frederick Fraser House

1803-04

This tall brick house is covered with stucco scored to simulate blocks. Double stairs over a wide arch lead to a piazza whose six slender fluted columns rise to meet those of a second floor verandah, both wide and high ceilinged. The sixteen-foot ceilings inside the house provide an atmosphere of lightness and airiness. A pretty Palladian doorway opens into the upper verandah, and a window of the same style provides light for the stair landing. The house has wide plank floors of heart-pine throughout, tall recessed windows, lovely beadwork trim on the high wooden mantels, dentil trim, and "piano key" cornice. The walls are eighteen inches thick. The tabby foundation arches have been bricked in.

In the old days this was one of the aristocratic neighborhoods in Beaufort. West Street, which borders the Fraser house, was the most important street running north and south, and the Fraser, Cuthbert, Barnwell and Bythewood families lived here.

Frederick Grimke Fraser built his house shortly after the turn of the nineteenth century. He was the grandson of John Fraser, a Scottish immigrant who settled on plantations in Pocataligo and Coosawhatchie in 1700.

14. 803 Prince Street

1700's

In danger of demolition, this house was moved by the Historic Beaufort Foundation to its present location. For the move, the porches were taken down but have been saved.

Originally the house had a center hall with two rooms on each side. An Adam motif is seen around upper and lower front doors. Under the eaves of the hip roof there are dentils.

15. 801 Prince Street

The Miles Brewton Sams House.

Pre Civil War

It is believed that Miles Brewton Sams built this house at an early date.

When the Victorian trimmings which had been added were removed, the typical Beaufort-style house appeared with old chimneys, six-over-six windows and double piazzas.

The house has been restored.

16. 711 Prince Street

The Daniel Hingston Bythewood House
circa 1792

Daniel Hingston Bythewood, a British merchant and sea captain, built this clapboard house for his wife, Elizabeth Taylor. She had persuaded him to relinquish his prosperous voyaging and become a Baptist missionary. In this profession he also served as supply minister for the Beaufort Baptist Church. Both he and his wife are buried in the Baptist churchyard.

Built upon a high tabby foundation and braced by sturdy chimneys, the house looks out over a long sweep of lawn. The outstanding paneled interior includes hand-carved mantels and over-mantels, chair rails and wainscoting. Original wide pine flooring still exists in all rooms. The single thickness of the interior walls is typical of early Beaufort and is one of the few examples left.

Turn right on Carteret then turn right again on North)

17. 902 North Street

Bythewood House

1897

Built in 1897 by a Bythewood and owned by descendants until 1974, this house has been remodeled into two suites of offices. It is a good example of adaptive use of former residences which have found themselves encroached upon by the business district.

At the corner of North Street and Harrington, look down Harrington to right for next house.

18. 509 Harrington Street

This home is an example of the Charleston-style of architecture. The structure borders the property line on two sides with a door from the street opening on the lower of two piazzas.

Left vacant for some years, the house was purchased and beautifully restored in the 1970's.

Continue on North Street

19. 1411 North Street

The Emil E. Lengnick House

circa 1900

Set at an angle so that the Beaufort River breezes could be enjoyed, this house was built by Emil E. Lengnick around 1900. Since that time there have been no substantial changes and there have been only two owners.

The house, Queen Anne vernacular style, is of heart pine construction with imbricated shingle siding. The turret with its steeply pitched roof shows the Gothic influence on the eclectic Victorian architectural period.

Turn left on Monson Street
then left on Bay Street

20. 1411 Bay Street

The E. A. Scheper House

1893

E. A. Scheper built a Victorian house on this lot in the 1890's, when, with its intricate lace and gingerbread exterior, it was a show place of Beaufort. A fine iron fence surrounds the house.

In 1938 the house was bought and almost completely rebuilt, transforming the exterior from Victorian to antebellum. The rooms were enlarged and the finest cabinetmakers were brought to Beaufort to make the beautifully carved mantel in the library and to cut and place the random-width flooring and paneling.

21. 1405 Bay Street

The Edward Barnwell House

1785

This frame house of excellent massing with fine chimneys and a well-proportioned portico, was built by Edward Barnwell, the father of sixteen children, the last of whom was nicknamed Sally Sixteen. Edward Barnwell was the great-grandson of "Tuscarora Jack" Barnwell, the Indian fighter.

During the Civil War Federal officers used the house for their quarters. They flattened one of the chimneys and erected a large platform on the roof from which the signal officer could send messages to the naval vessels anchored down the river.

The interior has two excellent paneled rooms with Adam-style mantels, good woodwork and a handsome Palladian window at the stair landing.

In the early 1900's actress Maude O'Dell lived here. Later in the 1950's the original slender columns and two piazzas were removed and replaced by Doric columns which rise to the roof unimpeded.

22. 400 Wilmington Street

(Facing Bay Street)

The John Joyner Smith House

circa 1811

Because John Joyner Smith and his wife disagreed as to where the entrance should be placed, this house has a false front door facing the river and a real entrance fronting on Wilmington Street. The lower parts of the windows on the first level open like doors to provide entrance to the porch. The roof is supported by large columns, made of brick, which extend all the way to the ground. The interior has handsome plaster cornices and woodwork. Wide doors allow the two front rooms to open into each other.

During the Civil War, General Stevens, the Federal Military Commander, occupied the house with his staff. His aide, William Thompson Lusk, wrote his mother during the war that "we are now pleasantly living in Beaufort with all sorts of comforts at our disposal. The house occupied by General Stevens is the one belonging to Mr. Smith and is an extremely elegant one. The portrait of Bishop Elliott looks down benignly from the mantel while I write. Personally I wish the owners were back in their homes." Stephen Elliott, to whom Mr. Lusk refers, was a bishop of the Episcopal Church.

The Smith house, like many other Beaufort homes, was used as a hospital during the Civil War.

The charmingly restored smaller house at the back of the property is believed to be the original barn or carriage house because of its hand-hewn beams and other interior details.

23. 1307 Bay Street

The William Ritchie House

circa 1883

Sitting primly and at ease amid its more imposing antebellum neighbors is this sturdy Victorian house. It was built about 1883 by William Ritchie, a foot soldier from Connecticut who came to Beaufort with the Northern Army and decided to remain. In its ninety or so years of existence, it has been on the market only once.

24. 1305 Bay Street

circa 1900

General Stephen Bull, a contemporary of "Tuscarora Jack" Barnwell, built a one-story cottage on this lot because he feared that a two-story structure could not withstand the strong winds and storms of the area. The present house, built on the original foundations in the early 1900's is surrounded by a fine well-preserved cast-iron fence made from Swedish ore. The lovely garden in the rear of the house was landscaped in the early 1950's.

25. 1301 Bay Street

The Leverett House

Pre-Revolutionary

This is a pre-Revolutionary house which was moved to this location from St. Helena Island by Dr. Benjamin Rhett around 1850. Charles Edward Leverett purchased it for $1,800 in 1854.

After the Civil War, Reverend Leverett, the last rector of Old Sheldon Church, wrote from Columbia the following letter to General Saxton:

"Sir, I am the owner of a home in Beaufort, the 5th from the west end of the Bay — and a plantation on the Main, one mile from Garden's Corner on the lower road to Pocotaligo, on the right hand side across and bordering Huspah Creek. From the latter place, I was ordered by the Confederate picketry. I have taken the oath required by the U.S. and now write to claim my property. Colonel Ely informed me that I was to address you and said there would not be the least difficulty in my recovering the home. I am an Episcopal clergyman and have been in the exercise of my dismal engagements throughout the war at this place. Will you inform me in regard to the above. You are aware that we cannot, on account of the climate, return to our places until after frost, and then I do not know in consequence of what I hear of the occupation of the Negroes, if it would be possible at that time. You will oblige me, General, by addressing a letter to me stating if I can have my two homes and land. I am, respectfully your Obt. Svt., Charles Edward Leverett."

More fortunate than most fellow townsmen, he regained ownership of his home after it had been confiscated during the war, and it remained in his family until 1920. The front door still retains its original lock, and for protection from high winds and intruders, a large wooden bar is set in iron brackets on the inside of the door.

26. 1211 Bay Street

The Thomas Fuller House. "Tabby Manse"
1786

Tabby Manse contains its original eight perfectly proportioned rooms, including three completely paneled in heart-pine and cypress. It has excellent Adam-style mantels, a superbly crafted stairway, a fine Palladian window in the rear elevation and a paneled second-floor drawing room. The hand-hewn major structural timbers measuring twelve inches thick, even in the attic, span the entire forty-five foot depth of the house, and are secured by large wooden pegs. Its two-feet thick exterior walls are made of tabby, an early local building material composed of oyster shells and lime mortar, finished with smooth stucco.

Thomas Fuller, its builder, was married to Elizabeth Middleton in 1786. He was a prominent Low Country planter.

One of their seven children, Richard Fuller, was a well-known mid-nineteenth century Baptist minister who built the Baptist Church in Beaufort. When Richard Fuller got the call to religion he gave a final boisterous party for his friends, during which he made a speech repudiating all his wordly ways in favor of the spiritual path.

The Onthanks and the Greenwoods operated *Tabby Manse* for many years of this century as a distinguished guest house, making it widely known and appreciated among artists, writers and architects.

Tabby Manse is considered to be one of the finest early houses in Beaufort.

27. 1207 Bay Street

The Robert Means House

circa 1790

When peace and prosperity returned to the Sea Islands after the disruption of the Revolution, Robert Means, a prominent merchant and planter, built this home on the Beaufort bay. It has a well-proportioned two-story verandah, a high arcaded basement, double entrance stairs, good chimneys with arched caps. The front door with a lovely fan light still retains its original lock. The house is built of cypress and is supported by hand-hewn major structural timbers ten inches thick. The main support is fifteen inches thick.

The original columns were replaced by Edwin Denby, Secretary of the Navy under President Harding, who owned the house from 1919 to 1928.

The wide entrance hall has a drawing room on the right, a dining room on the left. These rooms are completely paneled in heart-pine. Each has Adam-style mantels and original molding. A mahogany stair rail with slender balusters leads to a landing and a sitting room, then continues to two bedrooms on the second floor.

A Palladian window overlooks a garden of camellias and azaleas in the rear.

28. 1203 Bay Street

The John A. Cuthbert House

circa 1810

This fine Bay Street house has excellent interior and exterior woodwork. One front room has hand carved wainscoting and interesting hand carved doors. An old photograph shows this house with a double portico, each with delicate columns showing the Adam influence. While the house has been added to considerably, notably the porches and bay windows, it has retained its excellent proportions and is important to the Bay Street scene.

The legend concerning the early site of this house is that it was near Wyers Pond, but after much sickness and several deaths, the family decided that the location was unhealthy and had the house sawed in half and moved to its present site.

In a book written by an aide of General W. T. Sherman called *Marching With Sherman*, we find this information:

"The General came to Beaufort on the 23rd of January and stayed one day quartering at General Saxton's. The latter owns the house he lives in — a large fine double house on Bay Street fronting the sea. He bought it at one of the U. S. Tax Sales and I was told gave $1,000 for it."

29. 1103 Bay Street

The William Elliott House. "The Anchorage"

Pre-Revolutionary

It is recorded that the lot on which the house stands was originally granted to Samuel Wilson and John de LaGaye in 1753.

The house was built before the Revolutionary War by William Elliott I. Just prior to the Civil War it was lived in by William Elliott III, a remarkable man well-known as an agriculturist, author, sportsman, politician and poet. He was one of the most respected men in the state, in spite of his unpopular political views. While he was violently pro-Southern and in favor of slavery, he opposed Secession, and resigned his seat in the Senate rather than vote for Nullification. He regarded Robert Barnwell Rhett, leader in the Secession movement, as "unscrupulous" and "malignant." His was one of the voices of restraint heard in the town. He remained a staunch Unionist until the war broke out, when, like Lee, he went along with his state.

During the occupation of Beaufort the house was used as a hospital and designated as the Mission House. In 1876 the famous Confederate General, Wade Hampton, made a speech to the local citizens from its porch.

The house was greatly altered in the 1900's by a retired Naval officer, Admiral Beardsley. He spent $80,000 remodeling it, adding stucco to the exterior and much ornately carved woodwork to the interior. After his time, the house was used as a guest house for many years.

Threatened by demolition, "The Anchorage" was saved by Historic Beaufort Foundation, which, with the aid of a small group of friends, purchased the property. Subsequently resold, it is protected by a restrictive covenant.

Turn left on Charles Street.

30. 915 Port Republic Street

The Lucius Cuthbert House

circa 1820

This two-story frame house was the home of Lucius Cuthbert in 1820. Built over a high brick foundation, the original house was one room deep with two cypress paneled rooms and other rooms with wainscoting and plaster walls.

The Cuthberts refugeed to Aiken, South Carolina when the town was occupied and never again lived in Beaufort.

During the occupation the Federal Army used the house for a bakery.

Acquired in 1876 by F. W. Scheper, the house was changed by the addition of a second floor verandah, the cupola, the storm entrance and the handsome fence which bears the Scheper name.

The Victorian garden still retains its original plan including tiles marking the beds.

31. 308 Charles Street

"Woodbine Cottage"

Pre-Civil War

The date and builder of this house are unknown, but details of the construction mark it as very old. Once called "Woodbine Cottage," the house was originally a one-story building. It features dove-tailed sills and a foundation held together by wooden pegs.

General Rufus Saxton, sent to Beaufort as the first head of the Freedmen's Bureau in South Carolina, bought the house in 1864 at the U. S. Tax Commission sale. The upper story and verandah were added to the house in 1867.

End of Town Tour.

Tour of "The Point" and Carteret Street

Begin at the Bridge and Drive East on Bay.

32. 611 Bay Street

The Wallace House
1907

Dr. Thomas Fuller, son of Thomas Fuller, who built the *Tabby Manse,* once lived in a tabby house which stood on this corner. At one time fifteen children who all reached maturity lived in each of the three houses that originally stood on this block, making a total of forty-five. The Fullers, the Elliotts and the Samses had one hundred servants between them. After building the sea wall (which still stands here) the three families deeded the lots in front of their houses to the city, with the provision that nothing would ever be built on them.

The first two houses on the block burned in the great fire of 1907. The fire started when two young boys went down to the old MacDonald Wilkins wharf, where the Lady's Island bridge now crosses the Beaufort River, to smoke some forbidden cigarettes. When they heard footsteps approaching, they panicked and threw the incriminating cigarettes away, but, as fate would have it, the burning butts fell into a hay wagon. A high wind soon sent flames raging across the whole central part of Beaufort, destroying some of the town's finest homes.

The present house, built in 1907 after the fire, has excellent Victorian millwork typical of the period.

An attractive boutique is housed here.

33. 607 Bay Street

The William Joseph Thomas House
1909

Originally on this site was a very old tabby house built by an Elliott. This house was torn down and replaced by a clapboard dwelling which burned in the fire of 1907.

The present house was built in 1909 and is a fine solid Victorian structure. It was built by William Joseph Thomas of concrete stone blocks which had been made near the house from special materials brought by boat from Charleston. At the time the house was erected, the columns of concrete reinforced with steel across the front were said to be the second longest in the world.

34. 601 Bay Street

The Lewis Reeve Sams House

1852

This handsome Beaufort Style house has excellent exterior woodwork, Ionic columns over Doric on the verandahs, fine doorways and chimneys, and marble front stairs. The interior includes black marble mantels and excellent plaster work.

In the antebellum days there was no drinking water on this place, and accounts remain of processions of Negro children going back and forth to a well a quarter of a mile away, bringing water for the household.

The Union troops used the house as a hospital during the war. After the war Richard and Thomas Sams, sons of Lewis Reeve, recovered their home, a rare stroke of fortune for Beaufort residents during that period. In 1869 they sold it to George Waterhouse, a New Englander who came to Beaufort in 1864 to open a general store on Bay Street.

The house survived the great fire of 1907 when residences for two blocks west of it were completely destroyed. It was saved by the efforts of the Waterhouse cotton gin workers who formed a bucket brigade from the hand-pump in the kitchen to the upstairs windows and used wet blankets to beat out the flames.

In the backyard a small one-room house with a fireplace was used as a wash house.

Today this restored antebellum home is a bed and breakfast inn.

35. The Lot at the East End of Bay Street

Formerly the Property of the Gold Eagle Tavern

Michael Brewton was given this lot by grant. His grandson, Robert, sold it to Daniel DeSaussure who had come to Beaufort from Pocataligo.

Daniel DeSaussure's son, Henry William, had an illustrious career. He served in the Revolution and became a friend of General George Washington. Later he was asked by President Washington to become the first Director of the U.S. Mint. After he had been asked to coin gold, he carried to the President, in only six weeks, a handful of gold eagles. In 1798 Henry William DeSaussure became one of the chancellors of the state.

The present contemporary home was built on the foundation of the Gold Eagle Tavern, built in the 1930's.

36. 500 Port Republic Street

The George Mosse Stoney House

circa 1823

In the John Campbell painting of 1798 a house is shown on this lot. Bought by Dr. George Mosse Stoney, the house was replaced to please his wife, Sarah Barnwell. Dr. Stoney (1795-1854) practiced medicine.

An exposed beam in the rear upper hall indicates the house was originally one room deep. Also found in recent remodeling were hand-forged nails, mortised corners of clapboard and wooden pegs in sills.

The present house is beautifully proportioned with upper and lower porches on three sides, each supported by fourteen Doric columns and each finished with denticulated trim on the rooflines.

The inviting interior has a large hall, formal drawing and dining rooms and a beautifully paneled library.

Look to your extreme right for this house.

37. 212 New Street

The William Waterhouse House

1898

Built in 1898 by William Waterhouse as a wedding gift for his wife, Isabelle Richmond, this typical Late-Victorian style house has spacious piazzas on two sides. The upper piazzas were later added.

38. 214 New Street

The Thomas Hepworth House

circa 1717

The Oldest House in Beaufort

Thomas Hepworth, Chief Justice of the Colony, built this clapboard cottage on an original grant in the days when the Yemassee Indians were still a threat to the settlers.

The house is an early Colonial two-story cottage with a side porch. Its roof lines are simple gables broken by side dormer windows. The thick tabby foundation is pierced on the north side with slots locally said to be rifle slots. The floor sills are hand-hewn from whole trees adzed to 16 inches. The chimney is seven feet square set on a footing but finished to give the appearance of four chimneys.

The interior has some fine details emphasized in the corner cupboard and mantels.

Speaking of the War of Revolution as it affected Beaufort, Dr. John A. Johnson says "The only remaining memorials of that war within our present view are the two redoubts in the north-western suburbs and the little Dutch house on the corner of Port Republic and New Streets." Further he writes "At the close of the last century (eigh-teenth) an early cotton gin was invented and the first one was exhibited in the large front parlor of the antiquated Dutch-looking building at the south-west corner of New and Port Republic Streets, to the moderns known as Republican Headquarters."

In the early 1800's William Fickling conducted a private school for boys in this house.

39. South East Corner of New and Port Republic Streets

Pre Civil War

On these four corners stood the four oldest houses in Old Beaufort, local historians say. The four lots were land grants made in August 1717.

Land grant 49 gave this property to Peter Palmeter. The very old house which still stands is said to have been built by Taylor McKee. Originally a hallway separated two rooms on the first floor. On the second there were three bedrooms.

A lovely Adam-style mantel removed from the "Anchorage" when it was remodeled was brought by the former owner of the "Anchorage" to her new home where it now graces the drawing room.

The east end of the house is a much later addition.

40. 601 Port Republic Street

Pre Civil War

The property on which this small house stands was first granted August 8, 1717 to Francis La Basseur. In 1759 Philip Martin Angelo owned it. During the War Between the States it was sold at the tax sale of 1863 for one hundred dollars.

The quaint white clapboard house with its two-storied porches faces south toward the river.

Originally two rooms deep, upstairs and down, the house has been enlarged by the addition of a wing in the rear.

This charming small house is probably one of the oldest in town.

41. 310 New Street

The Berners Barnwell Sams House

1818

Built by Dr. Berners Barnwell Sams with slave labor in 1818, this white clapboard house has been occupied by the same family for four generations.

Typical of a Beaufort planter's summer home, built high from the ground, the house originally had six rooms and was only one room deep. Across the front were double piazzas with slender columns. On the roof was a parapet.

Several changes were made by the next owners. The parapet was removed and six rooms were added. These additions, however, gave the house interesting symmetry when viewed from Craven Street.

A two-room servant quarters with an addition stands nearby.

The entrance hall contains a curving stairway with platform landing. Fine dentil molding, cornices, wainscoting and Adam-style mantels decorate the two front rooms.

During the War Between the States the house was confiscated and used as Contraband Hospital No. 10. (Contraband was the term used for slaves.)

Make a right turn on Craven Street.

42. 509 Craven Street.

Early 1900's

In the early years of this century, Mr. Hare built this house over the burned foundations of a small antebellum dwelling. This property remained in his hands until the 1950's when it was purchased and altered extensively. From condemned eighteenth and nineteenth century Savannah residences came ceiling moldings, window frames, mantels, and lumber. Bricks to buttress existing foundations were purchased from the Trenholm School in Charleston, and Robert E. Marvin of Walterboro was commissioned to design a parterre garden behind the house using bricks from the old Savannah City Market, then being demolished. The circular stairway and the front portico are replicas of those in an early nineteenth century Charleston home and lend to the house the appearance of the Federal "raised cottage" type of architecture, found not only in the lowcountry but also in French inspired dwellings of the same style along the Gulf Coast and in the lower Mississippi Delta.

43. 506, 508, 510 Craven Street

This is a small section of Craven Street which is being restored into one of the most charming parts of town.

From about 1870 to the early 1900's the Victorian Age of architecture flourished. Ingenious wood working machinery had been invented which created ornate towers, turrets, bay windows, gables, shingles, bulging spindles, and portholes of colored glass.

Today these Victorian houses are being appreciated and preserved.

44. 507 Craven St.

This section of Craven Street has become one of the most charming parts of old Beaufort.

From about 1870 to the early 1900's, the Victorian age of architecture flourished. New wood working methods had been developed which created ornate towers, turrets, bay windows, gables, shingles, bulging spindles, and port-holes filled with colored glass.

The Craven Street houses were built in the 1870's to 1890's. Several are almost identical. All have decorations of the wood working machinery newly invented. Several have turrets and towers; some have colored glass; most have decorative spindles; a number have bay windows; several have nice piazzas. The owners have added to the charm of the street by using a variety of colors of paint on their houses.

Turn left on East Street

45. 411 Craven Street

The Joseph Johnson House. "The Castle"

circa 1850

Dr. Joseph Johnson completed this house except for marble mantels, ironwork, and stairs for the rear entrance before the start of the Civil War.

The house is Italian Renaissance in feeling, and said to be almost an exact copy of one in England, destroyed during World War II. Constructed on a crib of palmetto logs, the walls are of soft brick made in Dr. Johnson's brickyard on Lady's Island, and covered with a thin layer of plaster. The color is muted and changeable, in shades of gray, tan, and pink, subtly shifting with the light. Six massive columns support the double portico, with balusters between enclosing the upper and lower porches. The decorated parapet is five feet high, with four triple chimneys towering above it. Long French windows, some of the seventy-nine windows in the house, flank the front doors, upstairs and down. The interior walls are solid brick, plastered, and the double stairway is one of the widest in the country. Some of the original mantels have been replaced by Regency ones rescued from an old Beaufort house being demolished.

The house, one of the most photographed in America, occupies a full city block and is set amid lush gardens with hundreds of azaleas and camellias. It faces a great bend in the Beaufort River, and giant live oaks guard the front and back. Many of the specimin trees and shrubs in the garden were planted by Dr. Johnson, including a pair of ancient olive trees, brought from the Mount of Olives in the Holy Land.

A former director of the National Trust called it "One of the great houses of the South Carolina coast." He speaks of "the extraordinary grandeur of the almost medieval house . . . its air of somber mystery, set in great oaks at the water's edge."

46. 311 East Street

Pre Civil War

This is a white clapboard house with large, hand-hewn supporting beams seven feet above ground level. It stands on an inlet of the river. In the interior, one can see remains of ceiling cornices. In the centers of the two plaster medallions of grade design, there are iron hooks that once held chandeliers.

The builder and date of construction are unknown, but there are records to show that this house is an antebellum house.

47. 412 East Street

The Henry Farmer House

circa 1810

This early nineteenth century house with double galleries set on a high tabby foundation once overlooked the Beaufort River across the lot where *The Castle* now stands. The interior features fine wainscoting and carved cornices, marble mantels, and an excellent stairwell in the front hall. Wooden pegs and imported copper nails contribute to the structural soundness of the house.

Henry Farmer sold his house to the widow, Charlotte Beadon. Mrs. Beadon was involved in a law suit over Cat Island, and Richard Fuller acted as her lawyer, winning both the case and the widow.

The Fullers were both lovers of flowers, and when Dr. Fuller travelled abroad in the 1830's he returned with a number of imported specimens for their garden, most notably the Roman laurel and Guernsey lily (nierne), along with the Italian marble mantel for the drawing room. He built the lace brick wall around the house and enclosed the upper portion of the double portico for use as an upstairs study, where he pursued his varied vocations.

During the Civil War the house was used as a Federal hospital.

Turn left on North Street.

48. 507 North Street

The Gustave Sanders House.

It is not known who built this Victorian house in the late nineteenth century but Gustave Sanders bought it in 1903 and members of his family have owned it since. The double front piazzas are supported by Doric-style columns. Victorian trim is found under the piazza eaves and on the double bay windows. There are arched glass panels with side lights around the front door.

The rooms are large with high ceilings and seven-foot windows. Large sliding doors connect two front rooms which have ceiling cornices and center medallions. A jib door opens onto the upstairs piazza.

49. 411 New Street

The Cunningham House

1886

The widow of Henry Young Cunningham built this house as a summer place in 1886. She also had a small school erected nearby. In later years the two buildings were combined. Surrounded by beautifully kept grounds, the house is still occupied by descendants of the builder.

50. 509 North Street

Hasell House

1852

Built in 1852 by Thomas Hasell as a "honeymoon cottage" for his bride, this restored house is one of only a few in Beaufort which retains its original parapet.

George Holmes, who married Mr. Hasell's daughter, bought the house soon after it was built. During the Civil War, it was used as a hospital.

In 1902 Captain John Foster bought it at an auction, and, like the original builder, presented it to his bride, Etta Cunningham Foster, as a wedding gift.

The house has three garret windows above the second level verandah and handsome marble mantels in the interior.

51. 414 New Street

The William Johnson House

circa 1776

This house, built by William Johnson about the time of the Revolution, had a large one-story verandah until 1960.

Each of the three upper rooms has three exposures. The simple stairway is the original, with treads worn thin. There are hand-carved ceiling cornices and mantels and fine woodwork.

Turn right on New Street

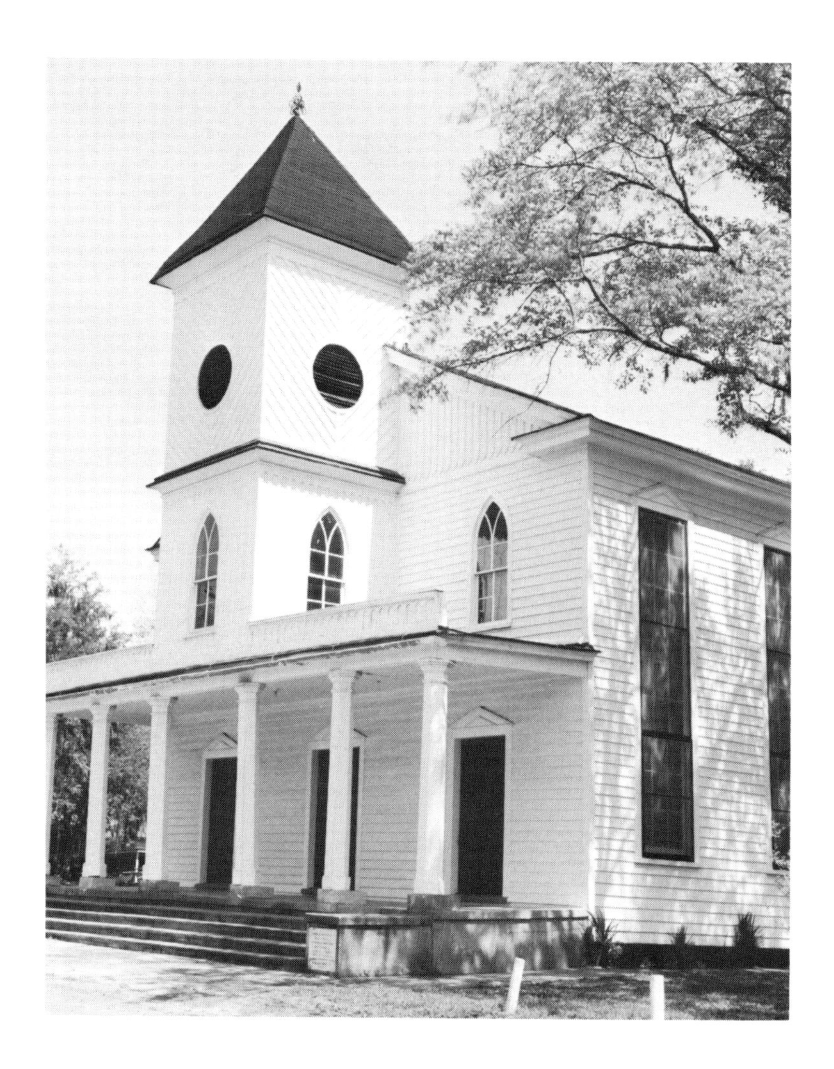

52. 601 New Street

First African Baptist Church
1865

The church was built in 1865 by freed slaves and given to other freed slaves. A marble plaque on the church states: "Presented as a token of respect by A. D. Deas to the first and present pastor, Reverend A. Waddell, of the First Baptist Church, a native of Savannah, Georgia, who became pastor of said church First of January 1865."

53. 608 Prince Street

On February 3, 1864 this house was sold at public auction by the United States Tax Commission for $450 to Hector Powell. The deed states that he "served as a volunteer in Company E, First South Carolina Volunteers, Army of the United States, for a full period of five months." This is the first record of the house. Construction indicates that it must have been built about twenty years before that, although the exact date is not known.

There were five different owners before it was restored in 1977. The original house had four rooms, each with a fireplace and heart pine floors. The fireplaces, floors, and two downstairs mantels are original. Several rooms were added during restoration.

54. 605 Prince Street

Pre Civil War

This attractive example of the Beaufort style small house has recently been restored. Facing south it has a center hall with rooms on each side, double porches, six over six windows, and covered interior chimneys.

In the rear the owner has developed a lovely rose garden.

55. 601 Prince Street

The Washington House
1912

During recent renovation, it became obvious that this house was originally one of the numerous six room houses built between 1840 and 1850, with four rooms on the main floor and two rooms upstairs, a fireplace in each room and no inside plumbing, piping or wiring. Water came from a well in the back yard, and cooking was done in a small separate cook-house. Later a one story extension was added under the same roof.

When Julius Washington bought the house in 1912 he added two upstairs rooms in back of the original two. He also reversed the stairs, so that they ascended from the rear of the central hall. This substantial house was owned by the Washington family until the 1960's.

56. 511 Prince Street

The Henry McKee House

1834

This large frame house with a two-story portico retains its original joiner-work and front entrance with trim. It is a typical house of the early period.

It has massive corner and diagonal timbers which didn't conserve wood but did conserve the house. A further means of sturdiness is that floor boards on the second floor are wider than on the first; this withstands the twisting action of a house in heavy wind.

Every room in the house has chair rails and dado. In the drawing room the Adam mantel extends to the ceiling and the pilasters of the mantel repeat the design of those of the front door.

Ceilings are twelve feet high, windows are eighteen panes, and all porches face south - cool in summer, warm in winter. The entire house has a very special welcome warmth of its own in all seasons.

Robert Smalls was born a slave in 1839 in one of the cabins which stood in the rear of the lot. He progressed from slave to pilot to army captain, National Guard general, legislator, congressman, and finally Collector of the Port of Beaufort. With prize money from the sale of the ship *Planter*, which he captured from Confederate forces at Charleston and delivered to Federal forces at Beaufort, he bought this house at a tax sale in 1863. The property remained in the Smalls family until 1940.

Henry McKee sold the house to the DeTreville family about 1855. The DeTrevilles sued to regain title of the house after the war and pursued the case all the way to the U. S. Supreme Court, which held Small's title valid. This test case decided the validity of all the wartime tax titles in South Carolina.

The McKees returned to Beaufort after the war, and Mrs. McKee, then quite old, wandered into the house one day thinking she was home. Robert Smalls installed her in her old room, and there waited on her as if she were still mistress of the house, until the day she died. Robert Smalls' remarkable life is chronicled in his biography, *The Captain of the Planter* by Dorothy Sterling.

This house was designated a National Historic Landmark in 1975.

continued on New Street

57. 712 New Street

Chaplin House
Pre-Revolutionary

This small Colonial story-and-a-half clapboard house is said to have been built by a member of the Chaplin family. Built throughout of heart-pine, the sills put together by wooden pegs, it originally consisted of the two large rooms on the first floor and two bedrooms in the dormered half story.

No definite date has been established as to the age of this house but several architects have estimated that it probably was built in the mid 1700's, maybe earlier. The marks of the adz are still plainly to be seen on the wide pine paneling on one wall of the two first floor rooms and on the floor-to-ceiling mantels. The original floors are of wide random-width pine in the two downstairs rooms and those in the upstairs rooms are at least twice as wide. Wainscoting is formed of 16 inch pine boards running horizontally. The chimneys are handmade random size brick with one chimney built several inches away from the house to lessen the fire hazard.

The kitchen was originally separate from the house but was later rolled up to it on logs. At the time the present owner bought the house in 1931, one entire wall of the kitchen consisted of a huge fireplace on which cooking was done. On the opposite side of the wall was a much smaller fireplace which heated a small room used as a hall into which five doors opened. One of these opens upon an enclosed narrow staircase leading to the upstairs rooms.

When this house was sold by the U. S. Tax Commission in 1863, it was bought by a newly freed woman. This family owned it continuously until the early 1930's.

58. 715 New Street

Pre Civil War

Originally two rooms over two, this house has had a wing added to the back. While its age is not known, the plaster-over-split lath walls, pegged rafters and hand-made nails suggest the mid-1800's. Neighbors remember a porch across the front. It could have been moved to its present location as part of the Robert Smalls estate.

Turn right on Duke, then right on East.

59. 712 East Street

Pre Civil War

This charming small house is thought by many to be one of the oldest houses in Beaufort. Formerly a center hall divided four rooms on the first floor. A narrow stairway led to two small dormer rooms. Recently the house has been enlarged and remodeled.

60. 409 Hancock Street

The Chaplin House

circa 1843

It is not known for whom the house was built in 1843 but a balustrade holds a pearl amity button inset (signifying complete agreement between the builder and owner) bearing that date. In 1860 John F. Chaplin purchased the house from John S. Fyler. Since that time the present owner and occupant is the third generation of the Chaplin family to have been married in this house.

This beautifully proportioned house is constructed with brick columns approximately eight feet apart resting on a tabby foundation supporting the main sills located at the second level. Wall studs are secured in the sills, both top and bottom, by mortise and tenon. The framework of mortised and doweled construction is principally heart-pine with random width flooring.

During the War Between the States the house was occupied by Union soldiers, some of whose names and regiments, written in chalk, can still be seen on the attic door.

61. 708 East Street

"The Tree House"

Moved to this location by the Robert Smalls family around 1910, the house previously was situated on the property known as Emmons farm at the corner of Carteret and Boundary.

When the present owner bought the property, she replaced the missing porches and added a small wing. The result is a charming house embracing its great oak and furnished with antiques in the manner of a New England farm house.

62. 502 Prince Street

"Pretty Penny"

1885

George Edward Doane built this small but pleasing house of simple Victorian architecture in 1885 of the choicest lumber from the lumber yard in which he worked. Each room has its own fireplace and wood closet.

Before the house was begun, the extremely low lot was filled in with palmetto logs to increase the elevation.

63. 501 King Street

The William Wigg Barnwell House

circa 1816

As recently as January, 1973, this house was slated for demolition. Through the intervention of Historic Beaufort Foundation several stays were granted and in September, 1973, it was moved from its original location at the southwest corner of Prince and Scott Streets to its present site.

The twelve room town house was built by the Gibbes brothers on behalf of their sister, Sarah Reeve Gibbes, who married William Wigg Barnwell. He was the grandson of the Revolutionary War hero, Major William Hazzard Wigg.

Over the years it has served as a school and as an apartment house. For the better part of this century it sustained much abuse and neglect. Despite this, much of the original paneling and a magnificent stairhall remained fairly intact.

Restored by a talented and experienced antiquarian, this house is an architectural asset and an example of what vision, courage and determination can achieve.

Opening from a wide entrance hall are four large rooms. The two front rooms are formal with wainscoting, marbelized mantels and antique English crystal chandeliers. The two at the rear have been adapted for modern living. On the second floor are three bedrooms, while on the third floor is a self-contained apartment reached by an elevator.

Turn left on King Street.

64. 411 King Street

The F. W. Sanders House

1910

Replacing a cottage that burned in the fire which swept through the town in 1907, the present two story house was built in 1910 of heart-pine with mahogany woodwork.

Surrounded by a spacious lawn, the house has ten large rooms and six fireplaces which give it an air of gracious living.

65. 401 King Street

"The Little Taj"

1856

This house, sometimes called "The Little Taj" due to the reflection of the house in the pool across the road, was built, according to the Courthouse records, in 1856. If unconfirmed sources are true, it must have been standing in 1823 when a Miss Jane Bond was married from the house to Henry McKee, for whom 511 Prince Street (the Robert Smalls House) was built.

A typical Beaufort small house, it was built to take full advantage of all breezes with porches at the front on both floors, and small wings to bring the breezes into the rear rooms. There are fireplaces, still useable, in all eight rooms with the old brick in place. Cutting into the rear wall recently to relocate an air conditioner, it was found the corner supports of the house are unsawn limbs of trees about six inches in diameter.

An old photograph shows the house after the great hurricane of 1893 without chimneys and porches.

66. 321 King Street

circa 1830

Little is known about this early nineteenth century house, but it is typical of many built in Beaufort during that period. Raised high off the ground on stuccoed piers, the front part of the house originally had two rooms upstairs over two down, with a shed extension on the north side. The two chimneys are stuccoed brick and stand free of the exterior walls. Three of the original mantels remain as well as the wide pine flooring in the north extension. About 1968 this house was restored from deplorable conditions. Although a few changes were made to the interior, the exterior retains its original contour.

Turn right on Hamilton Street then left on Federal Street.

67. 315 Federal Street

"Cassena"

Early 1800's

Thought to have been built in early 1800's by John Bythewood, whose daughter, Margaret, lived here with her husband, John Bell, before the Civil War. In 1863 it was bought by a former Bell slave, Mary Bell, sometimes called Mary Bythewood, who signed the deed with an "X". The house remained in the hands of former slaves and their descendants until it was severely damaged and abandoned after the storm of 1893. During the great storm boatloads of refugees from the islands were unloaded on the front porch of the house, the highest point in the vicinity.

In 1898, when Federal Street was still referred to as "Federal Alley," H. T. Danner, Sr. bought the house and repaired it.

Of the original Adam-style mantels, only one remains to suggest the former character of the house. Golden oak mantels, found in the house by its present owners have been replaced by fine Adam-style mantels and ceiling cornices. The size of the foundation beams, pegged rafters, and hand-made nails show the unusual soundness and age of the construction.

68. 310 Federal Street

"Moorlands"

Post Civil War

The original house on this site is shown in the 1798 sketch of the Beaufort waterfront done by John Campbell. Built by John Bell I and later sold to Robert Barnwell, the house was used as a hospital during the War Between the States. In the 1890's a great part of it was destroyed by fire. The present house was built on the original tabby foundation by Dr. Prioleau.

Facing south, upper and lower porches give a lovely view of the Beaufort River.

69. 302 Federal Street

The William Fripp House. "Tidewater."

circa 1830

This superbly designed, well-proportioned house was built in approximately 1830 by William Fripp, one of the richest planters in this area. Its two-story portico faces the river, and the excellent interior boasts a fan transom, a Palladian window, good mantels and carved plaster work.

William Fripp was the son of Captain John Fripp and Martha Scott Fripp. A family sketch of William by a great-grandson, Frampton Ellis of Atlanta, says this: "He was a polished scholar, an extensive traveler, and a thoroughly Christian gentleman. He was generous and open-hearted, a large part of his income being set aside for the poor of his county. In fact, so well known were his benevolences and purity of life that he was known all over the state as 'Good Billy Fripp.' "

The records of Beaufort District show that he owned nine plantations and 313 Negro slaves.

In May of 1820 William Fripp married Sarah Harriett Reynolds Prentiss, a widow with many possessions.

Like so many others, this house was sold for taxes during the Civil War.

70. 303 Federal Street

The James Rhett House

1884-1886

James Rhett began his house in 1884 when he was twenty-three years old, fully intending to make it two rooms deep. When he found that his finances would not support such an ambitious project, he changed his original plans and the house became known as "Rhett's Folly."

On each floor a center hall separates two large front rooms with twelve-foot ceilings. The downstairs rooms have elaborate cast plaster moldings and ceiling medallions. An arcaded masonry wall supports double verandahs across the front of the house. Wide bay windows extend the width of the parlor on the west. Jib doors give access to the porches and also add cross ventilation.

Turn left on Pinckney Street.

71. 501 Pinckney Street

The James Robert Verdier House.
"Marshlands."
circa 1814

The graceful waterfront home of Dr. James Robert Verdier provides a blend of Barbadian plantation architecture with the more formal Adam features of the Federal period. Set high off the ground and supported by arches, the exterior of the house shows the Barbadian influence in the single porch that runs across the front and around the sides of the house where it joins the back rooms. Inside, the Adam motif prevails with the lovely mantels and the beautiful stairway lit by a Palladian window. The house also shows other fundamentals of Adam architecture with its easy communications and balanced proportions.

Dr. Verdier treated with some success yellow fever and helped mitigate the horrors of an epidemic in the area.

During the war years, the house was used as the headquarters of the U. S. Sanitary Commission.

Marshlands is the imagined home of Emily, the heroine of Francis Griswold's novel of the Civil War, *Sea Island Lady*.

In 1975 the James Robert Verdier House was designated a National Historic Landmark.

72. 604 Pinckney Street

The Edward Means House

circa 1853

Colonel Edward Means built this brick mansion with a fine two-story verandah shortly after 1853. Entered from the end elevation facing east on the "The Green," the interior of the house is notable for its spacious quality. It has fine woodwork, marble mantels, and a beautiful floating spiral staircase. Like almost all Beaufort antebellum houses, the porch faces south to receive prevailing breezes, sun in winter and shade in summer.

A special war correspondent sent the following dispatch to the *New York Daily Tribune* in December, 1861: "The splendor of the houses and furniture and the beauty of the place may have been exaggerated, but the house of Colonel Edward Means would be called handsome in any town in the North."

Turn right on King Street, look across "The Green" for next house.

73. 207 Laurens Street

1907

In the late nineteenth century the front of this attractive house was the paymaster's office at the Coosaw Mines on Lady's Island. After the mines closed, it was moved in 1907 by lighter across the river to the end of Pinckney Street. From there it was rolled on logs to its present location and combined with an old house on Hancock Street.

Continue around "The Green" for the next house.

74. 100 Laurens Street

The Paul Hamilton House. "The Oaks"
circa 1856

This Italianate style house set in the shade of magnificent oaks is of frame construction on a brick foundation. The wide porches extend across the front of the house and continue around the sides to meet the projecting back rooms which have bay windows rising from the floor almost to the ceiling. The house has unusual carved mantels that extend around the sides of the chimneys.

Built in 1856 by Colonel Paul Hamilton, the grandson of Paul Hamilton, Secretary of the Navy under President Madison, the house was deserted by the family in 1861 when Beaufort was occupied by Federal soldiers.

When the house was auctioned in November 1865, Colonel Hamilton declared that he would bid up to a million dollars to save his home from becoming a school for Negroes. The Colonel obtained an option on the house with payment to be made within three days, this period allowing for a boat trip to Charleston to secure funds. On the second day, however, the Colonel's young son ran home with the news that the house would be sold at sunset. Mr. George Holmes, a northern merchant, led other indignant citizens in hastily raising the money before sunset and the house was bought in the name of Colonel Hamilton.

75. 201 Laurens Street

The Berners Barnwell Sams House No. 2
1852

Dr. Berners Barnwell Sams built his house of brown-toned plantation brick with four sturdy brick Doric pillars supporting a flat roof with a balustrade around the top. These columns support a two-story verandah and give the house a handsome, massive look. It has excellent brickwork, good chimneys, and fine interior details including marble mantels in the front rooms. Facing an open area which is part of the property and long known as the "front green," the Sams house is a fine example of Classic Revival architecture.

The dependency, which has been converted into attractive apartments, contained a blacksmith shop, a cook house with a great fireplace, a laundry, storeroom, and rooms for the household servants.

The house was used as a hospital during the Civil War. It was bought by William Wilson at a U.S. Tax Commission sale and later served as St. Helena's rectory, housing the Reverend A. P. Hay, the "poet of the Confederacy."

Since 1895-96 this house has been owned by descendents of George Crofut.

Look to the right for Tidalholm.

76. 1 Laurens Street

The Edgar Fripp House. "Tidalholm"
circa 1856

Edgar Fripp built this large Italianate style frame house as his summer home, when the heat and mosquitoes made life in his plantation home on St. Helena Island intolerable. His brother, James Fripp, owned the house at the time of the Civil War. When James Fripp returned after the war, he arrived just as the house was being sold for taxes by the U. S. Tax Commission. The legend is that, unable to bid on the house, he stood with tears coursing down his cheeks. A Frenchman, who had been living in the area and who was sympathetic to the South, purchased the house. He is said to have walked over to the former owner, presented him with the deed, kissed him upon both cheeks, and left, returning to France before Mr. Fripp had a chance to repay him. A letter from the Frenchman is in the possession of the Fripp descendents verifying this story.

Used as a guest house from the 1930's to the early 1970's, "Tidalholm" brought to Beaufort as guests many artists, authors, professors, statesmen. It was instrumental in bringing many visitors who decided to make this town their home.

Set high off the ground in the center of an oak-shaded lot, the house is almost encircled by the Beaufort River. The wide entrance hall opens on two handsome rooms. The woodwork over the doors and windows is reeded with medallions at each corner. The distinctive plaster cornice resembles paper lace.

Restored in 1974 as a private residence, it has kept its air of charm and gracious living.

Turn left on Hancock.

77. 207 Hancock Street

The Elizabeth Hext House. "Riverview"
circa 1720

Set well back from the street on a high tabby foundation, the Hext house is considered to be one of the oldest houses in Beaufort. The original house consisted of upper and lower piazzas, a narrow central hall flanked by two rooms on the main floor, and a rear hall and staircase which led to two bedrooms upstairs. A quality of intimacy pervades the house due to its relatively small scale when compared to the houses of the later antebellum period. The two front rooms have wainscot paneling around three walls with floor-to-ceiling paneling on the exterior fireplace walls. Many of the windows have the original six-over-nine light panes and retain much of the old glass. The floor boards in all but the present kitchen and back hall are of ten inch wide first-growth pine planks. Interior walls are the thickness of only one plank, which indicates that the house is supported mainly by the exterior walls.

Elizabeth Hext, the only child of Francis Hext, Jr. and Elizabeth Stanyarne was born in 1746. At the age of fifteen she married William Sams of Wadmalaw Island, grandson of "Tuscarora Jack" Barnwell. In 1783 he bought Datha Island, near Beaufort, and here they lived and raised a large family.

When Elizabeth Hext Sams died in 1813, she was buried beside her husband on Datha Island. The Hext House remained in the Sams family until 1864 when it was sold for $640 by the U. S. Tax Commission.

78. 804 Pinckney Street

The John Johnson House

circa 1850

Dr. John Johnson and his wife, Claudia Talbird, built this three-story Classic Revival style house in the 1850's. The two-story piazzas on the south side are fronted by classical columns, Doric below and Corinthian above. The eighteen-inch thick walls and the four massive interior chimneys are of unusually large brick. French casement doors open onto the piazzas. The main entrance is on the east side of the house with marble steps, rather than on the south where the piazzas are located.

This sophisticated town residence was built in a period of high prosperity, and planned for formal living on a grand scale. A suite of rooms opens to the piazzas, allowing for sun in winter, shade and southerly breeze in summer. There are front and rear interior stair halls, fireplaces topped with wood or marble, and marble mantels in every room. The wide flooring, molding, doors, and paneled window frames are of local heart-pine.

79. 313 Hancock Street

Talbird-Sams House

1786

Built in 1786 by Henry Talbird, this typical Beaufort house was later owned by Dr. Lewis Reeve Sams, Jr., who sold it to Thomas Talbird. Because the daughter of the owner married the son of another owner, the house is now lived in by descendants of both the Sams and Talbird families.

The interior has very fine wainscoting and dentil trim at the ceilings. The doors to the two front drawing rooms have their original rim locks, one with a five inch brass key which works! The upper floor is one room deep and originally had a Palladian window at the stair landing.

Turn right on Hamilton Street, left on Bayard Street.

80. 411 Bayard Street

The Reverend Thomas E. Ledbetter House
early 1800's

This excellent Beaufort style house has an unusually fine setting with a magnificent view of the river from the two-story verandah which extends halfway along two sides of the house. It has good inset chimneys, a fine hipped roof, handsome doorways, and other exterior detailing. The interior features eight mantels, good wainscoting, deep cornices, and an original ceiling medallion.

Mr. Ledbetter served as a minister to the Beaufort Methodist Mission for many years. This mission was an attempt to evangelize the slaves on the cotton and rice plantations.

In 1881 the house was purchased by Mr. Neils Christensen, Sr. who designed the garden and planted its many unusual trees and shrubs.

It is said that when Clara Barton, founder of the American Red Cross, came to Beaufort after the storm of 1893 she stayed in the Christensen home.

Empty some four years, this house has been beautifully restored by its owners.

Turn right on East Street,
then left on Washington Street.

81. 500 Washington Street

The Trescot House

circa 1860

(Insert picture made in 1932 on Bay Street)

William Henry Trescot, historian and diplomat, built this house on Barnwell Island Plantation, near Parris Island, shortly before the Civil War. He served as secretary of legation at London in 1852 until 1854 and was appointed assistant secretary of state by President Buchanan in 1860. Most of the construction of this frame house was done by Trescot's slaves with the window sashes, doors and paneling being done in Charleston.

Colonel William Elliott took the house down in 1876 and brought it by boat to Beaufort and erected it at 1011 Bay Street just as it had been on Barnwell Island.

Almost a hundred years later, in 1975, threatened with demolishment, the house was moved a second time and restored by its present owners.

82. 503 Washington Street

"Petit Point"

Pre-Civil War

All that is known of this small antebellum home is that it was built for the spinster sister of the Chaplin family and that it was sold in the Tax Sale of 1863. Originally there were only two upper and two lower rooms with a front and back piazza. The wing to the right is a recent addition.

Before its restoration this house was generally considered "too far gone." Now it is a prime example of the inherent charm of many of Beaufort's small houses.

Turn right on Carteret Street.

83. 701 Greene Street

The DeTreville House

circa 1780-85

Believed to have been built by the Reverend James Graham of Scotland who married Sarah Jane Givens of Beaufort, this frame house with tabby foundations has two fine exterior end-wall chimneys, good dormer windows, and other exterior detailing. The fine interior details include mantels, wainscoting, a mahogany staircase, and an original ceiling medallion in the drawing room.

In the mid-nineteenth century the Misses Fanny and Julia Baker lived in this house, which became known as the Baker house. Miss Julia was the author of the poem "Mizpah—God Watch Between Me and Thee," which was very popular during her day. The Misses Baker fled at the beginning of the Civil War.

During the Reconstruction, the house became known as "The Mission" and was occupied by Mrs. Rachel C. Mather and the Baptist missionaries who built Mather School for the furtherance of Negro education and who were active in the Freedmen's Aid Society.

84. Carteret & Boundary

Conant House
circa 1870

This post-bellum house with its spectacular view of the river is a fitting introduction to the Historic District. Built of clapboard and distinguished by a mansard roof, the house is two-and-one-half stories tall. Double piazzas face south. Dormer windows face north, south, east and west.

John Conant of Bangor, Maine served as a captain in the 8th Regiment of Maine during the Civil War. After the war he returned to Beaufort, bought this property, tore down the small building on the site that had been used as a barracks during the war, and built this house. He brought his wife, Elvira and his only daughter, Lucy, to Beaufort to make their home. John Conant opened an ice house. Several times each year vessels came down from Maine bringing huge cakes of ice packed in sawdust.

For many years this was an inn known as "Bellamy Inn." Facing demolition in recent years, the house was purchased and completely restored. It is now an an attractive antique shop.

Turn left on Congress
Look right Conant House.
Turn left on Scott.
Turn left on Washington.

85. 705 Washington Street

Elizabeth Barnwell Gough House
circa 1789

The "Old Barnwell House" is one of a small group of Beaufort buildings based in their appearance on the Miles Brewton House in Charleston (c. 1765) and at a distant remove, the Palladian Villas of the Venetian mainland.

The house is "T" shaped; two storeys high raised on a basement. Construction is of tabby with the external finish scored to simulate stonework. Rooms and portico retain the generous proportions of the mid-eighteenth century, however the pervasive influence of the Adam and emerging Federal styles can be seen in slender upper porch columns, simple reeded pilaster of the main entrance and details of fireplaces and paneling.

The main reception area (ballroom) is on the second floor and is reached by way of a double stair. It is fully paneled in heart pine and cypress, retaining traces of an early painted colour scheme in blue and light tan. Thanks to the generosity of Mr. & Mrs. H. L. Pratt, III, paneling removed from the lower S.E. room in the 1930's has been returned as a gift to the Foundation.

Elizabeth Barnwell was the granddaughter of Tuscarora Barnwell. She married Richard Gough of James Island in London during 1772. Their only child Marianna was born in 1773. After a bitter quarrel Richard and Elizabeth separated. Following the death of Elizabeth's father in 1775, Edward Barnwell built the house with money left for her benefit.

Marianna married James Harvey Smith in 1791. Their six sons changed their name to Rhett. One son, Robert Barnwell Rhett, who may have been born in the house, grew up to be called "Father of the Secession."

Turn right on Carteret Street.

86. 800 Carteret Street

The Old Beaufort College Building
1852

This unusual example of late Greek Revival architecture is simple, even severe, in its proportions. Details have been handled boldly, as is seen in the cornice and the simplicity of the belled column capitals, the only ornament being in the elaborate bracket of the pedimented entrance.

Erected in 1852 for a boys' school, the building was taken over during the Civil War by General Stevens, Federal Military Commander. Books from the college were taken by agents of the U.S. Treasury to New York. Some were being auctioned when Chief Justice Chase, formerly Secretary of the Treasury, ordered the sale stopped. The books were then taken to the Smithsonian Institution for safekeeping, but almost all of them were lost when a wing of the Smithsonian burned down.

The building was leased to the Freedmen's Bureau after the Civil War. It was later used as a private school, a public school, and now houses the administrative offices of the University of South Carolina, Beaufort Branch.

87. 802 Carteret Street

St. Peter the Apostle's Church

circa 1846

Catholicism in the area of Beaufort has a long and interesting history. Early Spanish settlers came in 1520 and with them Dominican missionaries who offered Mass on St. Helena Island.

By 1670 a Franciscan Mission constructed of tabby was built and for approximately ten years it was unmolested by the Indians.

The Church had a resurgence in Beaufort about the time Bishop John England was named Bishop of Charleston in 1820. Michael O'Conner, a devout Catholic from Ireland arrived in Beaufort in 1822. Finding no church here, he made arrangements to have Mass said in his residence by Father Edward Quigley on his regular visits to Beaufort.

Michael O'Conner later donated property for a church, and St. Peter the Apostle's Church was dedicated in November 1846 by Bishop Ignatius Reynolds. Father Jeremiah J. O'Connell was named the parish priest. It was remodeled in 1946, doubling its capacity. It is of wood construction, surrounded by a brick wall, which was built by Thomas and Franklin Talbird.

88. 602 Carteret Street

circa 1900

This is a charming example of Gothic architecture with small steeple, weather vane, fish scale siding and pointed arched windows.

Used as a black Presbyterian church for some time, it was purchased from the synod and became a library for the blacks of the county from 1932 to 1965.

Recently it has become the location for the Art Department of the University of South Carolina, Beaufort.

89. 409 Carteret Street

The John Barnwell Grant

1764

The original grant No. 139 was made to John Barnwell on July 18, 1764.

A small, very old house on this lot was remodeled in the 1900's into a two-story house with piazzas facing south. Unfortunately, nothing really is known about this attractive place. The 1863 tax sale map shows it was bought by a Rickenbacker for $600.

A successful example of adaptive use, it now houses a very popular fashion boutique.

90. *National Cemetery*
Boundary Street

One of the ten National Cemeteries established by President Lincoln in 1863 Fifty acres of land were enclosed by a brick wall.

The first burials were in 1863 from East Florida, Savannah, Charleston, Morris Island, Hilton Head and other islands nearby. At the end of the War Between the States there were 3,798 graves in the cemetery. Today there are 11,267. Of these 121 are Confederate and 4,018 unknown.

Additional Tour Information

"Open House" Tours of Private Homes, Churches and Plantations

In mid-October the Historic Beaufort Foundation conducts tours in private homes in Beaufort. For information about these tours contact Historic Beaufort Foundation or the Beaufort Chamber of Commerce.

In late March, St. Helena's Episcopal Church conducts tours of plantations and private homes.

The Chamber of Commerce also sponsors minibus tours of the Beaufort Historic District throughout the year.

County Excursion

Excursion No. 1.

Fort Frederick, Parris Island, Retreat Plantation — 26 miles round trip.

Take Ribaut Road to State Highway 281. Stop at Fort Frederick on the grounds of the Naval Hospital. Fort Frederick was built in 1732-34 for defense against the Spanish, French and Indians. By 1756 the fort had fallen into disrepair and was abandoned in 1758. Though partly destroyed, some of the tabby walls still stand.

Continue on Highway 281 to the historic little town of Port Royal where the first English colonists to settle in South Carolina landed in 1670 before deciding to move onward to settle Charleston.

Highway 281 leads to Parris Island, the U.S.M.C. Training Station for recruits. Visitors are admitted with due respect by the sentry at the gate.

In 1562 Jean Ribaut established the first Protestant settlement in the New World and built Charles Forte on the northeast side of the island. In 1926 the U.S. government erected a monument to Ribaut on this site.

There is evidence to indicate that the sixteenth century Spanish forts, San Filipe and San Marcos, once stood on Parris Island. In 1969 the Beaufort County Historical Society erected a marker describing the activity of the Spanish on the island.

Parris Island was designated a U.S. Naval Station in 1876 and continued as such until 1906 when it became a Naval prison. In 1915 the island was purchased and turned over to the Marine Corps for use as a training station for recruits. There is an excellent military museum which is open to the public.

After leaving Parris Island continue on 281 to the next main intersection where Route 280 forks to the right. Follow 280 about 3 miles. On your right is the entrance to Retreat Plantation, now a private home.

The only pre-Revolutionary plantation house in the county. Retreat was built about 1773 by Jean de La Gaye, a French Huguenot.

You may continue on Route 280 to the intersection with 170. Bear right here then right again on Highway 21 which will bring you back to Beaufort.

Excursion No. 2.

Gardens Corner, Sheldon Church Ruins, Tomotley Plantation — 17 miles one way.

Following U.S. 21 westward from Beaufort you come to the Marine Corps Air Station, formerly Barnwell Plantations of *Woodward* and *Laurel Bay*. Further along, Highway 21 meanders through salt marshes and crosses Whale Branch, eight miles from Beaufort. Whale Branch supposedly received its name when a whale found its way into the stream during high water and was trapped by the outgoing tide.

Fifteen miles from the City of Beaufort on your left is Dean Hall, an 1827 plantation house formerly located near Cypress Gardens, which was moved to this location and rebuilt brick by brick.

Sixteen miles from Beaufort is the junction of Highway 21 and U.S. 17. This crossroads is called Gardens Corner after Colonel Benjamin Garden who once owned a plantation at this point.

Turning south on U.S. 17 for approximately one-tenth of a mile, and then turning right on a paved road (marked S.C. 21) brings you after several miles of pleasantly shaded driving to the ruins of Sheldon Church. The ruins, where services are held each year on the second Sunday after Easter, are those of a church twice burned by invading armies. The first church was built on glebe lands in 1745-48. It was burned by the British during the Revolution, rebuilt, and burned again by General Sherman in 1865.

One mile further along U.S. 21 is the entrance to Tomotley Plantation. Though the property is private, visitors are allowed to drive through the entrance gates and down the moss-hung avenue of oaks bordering the dirt road. The antebellum rice plantation once consisted of 13,000 acres laid out in the Yemassee Indian lands. This was the original landgrant in South Carolina dating from 1696.

Excursion No. 3.

St. Helena Island, Dataw Island, Frogmore, Penn School, Chapel of Ease, Fort Fremont, Hunting Island, Fripp Island — 58 miles round trip.

St. Helena Island, five miles from Beaufort across the Lady's Island bridge on U.S. 21, is eighteen miles long and four to six miles wide. It was named Punta de Santa Elena by the Spanish explorers who came here in 1520.

Seven miles from Beaufort is the small settlement of Frogmore. Turn left one and one-half miles to the gate of Dataw Island, a recently developed club and residential community. In 1786, William Sams planted indigo on the island and built a tabby house and complex which was destroyed by fire in 1876. The ruins are being carefully restored by the developers. Turn right at Frogmore onto a paved road and go one mile to Penn School, established during the Civil War by Philadelphia missionaries, Laura Towne and Ellen Murray, as the first southern school to be opened for Negroes. On the left, as you enter the school grounds, is the Brick Church, which served all elements of the missionary community during the critical Reconstruction period. It was the center of political and educational as well as religious activities. Teaching a wide variety of subjects from agriculture to art and hygiene to home economics. Penn School for years has helped and influenced the Black community of the county. In 1975 Penn Center was designated a National Historic Landmark.

Continuing down this same road brings you to a fork. Turn right. On the immediate left are the ruins of the Chapel of Ease. Erected before the Revolutionary War as a convenience for the St. Helena Island members of St. Helena's Church in Beaufort, the chapel was burned in a forest fire after the Civil War.

Continue on County Road 45 for approximately 9 miles. A historical marker on your right indicates the road which leads to Fort Fremont, erected during the Spanish American War.

At *Lands End,* County Road 45 joins County Road 77, a sharp turn to the left. This will take you through a typical countryside of farm lands and small houses, belonging mostly to the island black people. *Tombee, Fripp Plantation* and *Frogmore Manor* are located in this area. The houses of *Tombee* and *Fripp* are the original structures. Continue straight down this road, cross Highway 21 and continue through an avenue of beautiful live oaks, which will bring you to *Coffin Point Plantation.*

Built in early 1800, it was owned by the Coffin family up to the Civil War. In 1860 it was acquired by Edward Philbrick, an engineer from Boston who came to Beaufort as part of the early reconstruction effort known as "The Port Royal Experiment." *Coffin Point* was the scene of the first and most successful effort to raise Sea Island cotton retaining the plantation system but using paid freedmen instead of slaves.

page

R

S

page

T/U

V

W/X/Y/Z

House Number

1. The George Elliott House
2. The John Cross Tavern Site
3. The Habersham House
4. The John Mark Verdier House
5. The Arsenal
6. The W. J. Jenkins House
7. The Tabernacle Baptist Church
8. The Thomas Rhett House
9. "The Rectory"
10. "Secession House"
11. St. Helena's Episcopal Church
12. The Beaufort Baptist Church
13. The Frederick Fraser House
14. 803 Prince Street
15. Miles Brewton Sams House
16. Daniel Hingston Bythewood House
17. 902 North Street
18. 509 Harrington Street
19. The Emil E. Lengnick House
20. The E. A. Scheper House
21. The Edward Barnwell House
22. John Joyner Smith House
23. The William Ritchie House
24. 1305 Bay Street
25. The Leverett House
26. "Tabby Manse"
27. The Robert Means House
28. The John A. Cuthbert House
29. "The Anchorage"
30. The Lucius Cuthbert House
31. "Woodbine Cottage"
32. The Wallace House
33. The William Joseph Thomas House
34. The Lewis Reeve Sams House
35. Former Gold Eagle Tavern.
36. George Mosse Stoney House
37. William Waterhouse House
38. The Thomas Hepworth House
39. New & Port Republic Sts.
40. 601 Port Republic Street
41. B. B. Sams House (New St.)
42. 509 Craven Street
43. 506, 508, 510 Craven Street
44. 507 Craven St.
45. "The Castle"

House Number

46. 311 East Street
47. The Henry Farmer House
48. The Gustave Sanders House
49. The Cunningham House
50. Hasell House
51. The William Johnson House
52. First African Baptist Church
53. 608 Prince St.
54. 605 Prince Street
55. The Washington House
56. The Henry McKee House
57. Chaplin House
58. 715 New Street
59. 712 East Street
60. The Chaplin House
61. "The Tree House"
62. "Pretty Penny"
63. The William Wigg Barnwell House
64. The F. W. Sanders House
65. "The Little Taj"
66. 321 King Street
67. "Cassena"
68. "Moorlands"
69. "Tidewater"
70. The James Rhett House
71. "Marshlands"
72. The Edward Means House
73. 207 Laurens Street
74. "The Oaks"
75. B. B. Sams House (Laurens St.)
76. "Tidalholm"
77. "Riverview"
78. The John Johnson House
79. Talbird-Sams House
80. Reverend Thomas E. Ledbetter House
81. The Trescot House
82. "Petit Point"
83. The DeTreville House
84. Conant House
85. Elizabeth Barnwell Gough House
86. The Old Beaufort College Building
87. St. Peter the Apostle's Church
88. 602 Carteret Street
89. The John Barnwell Grant
90. National Cemetery